Mother Earth
and a different
kind of friend

by Maureen Annette Russell

Illustrations by Laura Caiafa

i

Dedicated to all
Mother Earth's children,
including my dad Fredrick
and mum Sylvia.

♥

Mother Earth
and a different
kind of friend

Mother Earth was sure she had told snake to stop hiding in her long grass...

...humans, especially the children
had become very scared of
seeing his two heads.

Earth remembered when snakes had
only one head, she knew this snake
was different, and she had got
used to feeding both of his heads.

Lately though, the little children are scared to play on her soil and grass.

Earth told snake the children are
preferring to play on the concrete,
or to play indoors on the computers,
rather than swinging from trees,
or jumping on her soil.

This made Earth sad, she missed
the digging up of her soil for planting,
and the platting of her long grass.

Snake sadly knew it was now time
for him to leave...

...because Mother Earth just loves
her children, especially those
little ones on two legs.

If only Wind could blow by this minute and give him a big gush so he can get out of there, he was not one for staying where he was not wanted.

Snake remembered that Earth is always talking about her children, planning and growing gardens for them.

She even allowed the children
to lay on her while kissing her,
yuck thought snake.

Earth though was kind, beautiful and gentle, the opposite to him.

Snake Adder became more desperate,
he wanted Wind to blow by and
to hopefully carry him far away.

He was not looking forward to
moving in the afternoon heat,
but knew he had to.

Snake Adder grew worried,
the big humans might see him,
shoot at him or use Fire to burn him.

What use is it having two heads
he thought, if not to see clearer,
quicker, and smarter!

The thought made him feel much better.

Earth spoke again, "Snake you will have to find a new home far from here."

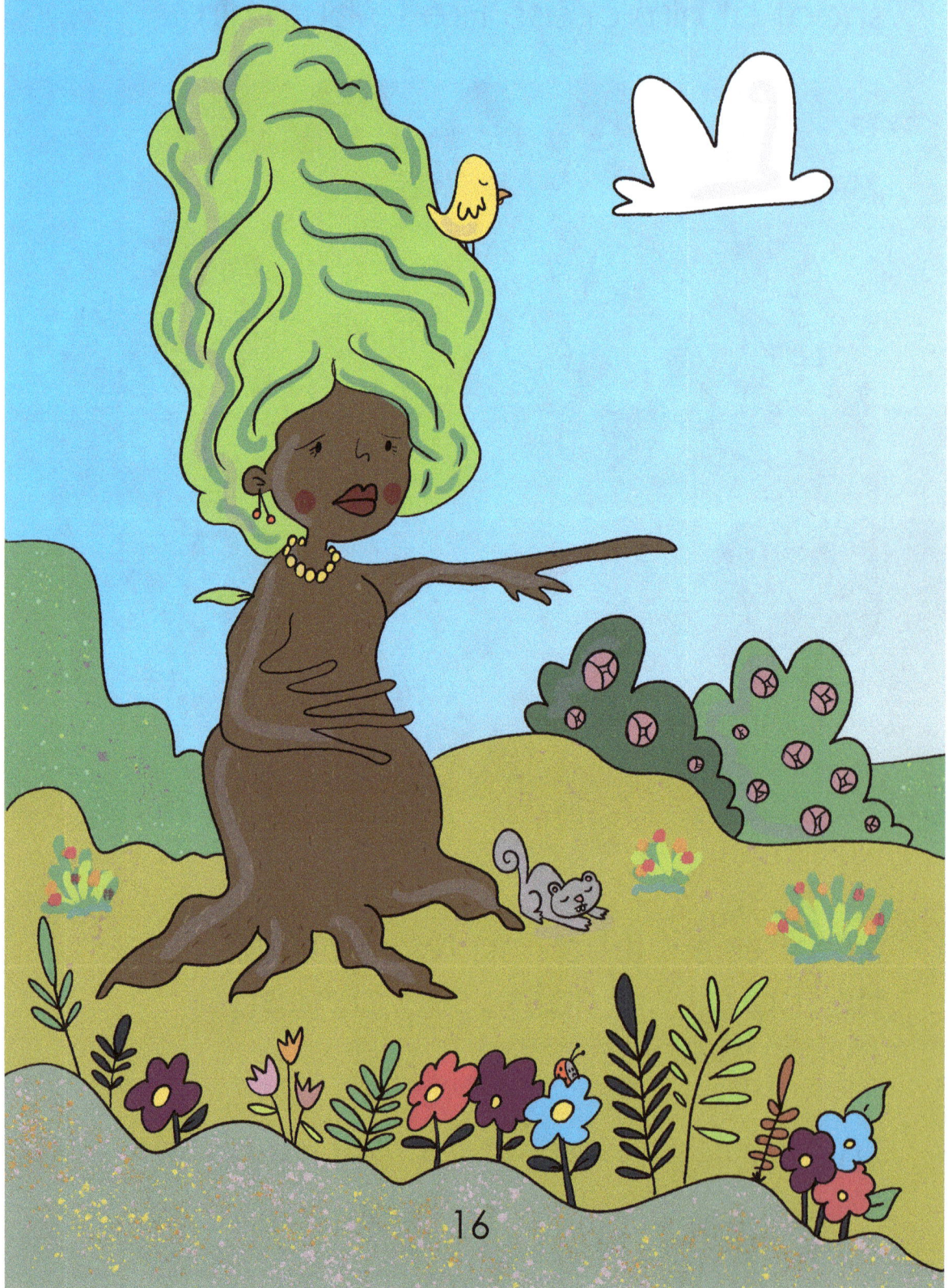

Snake Adder was not listening anymore, he was quietly thinking, and decided he was not going to wait around for Wind but would move by himself.

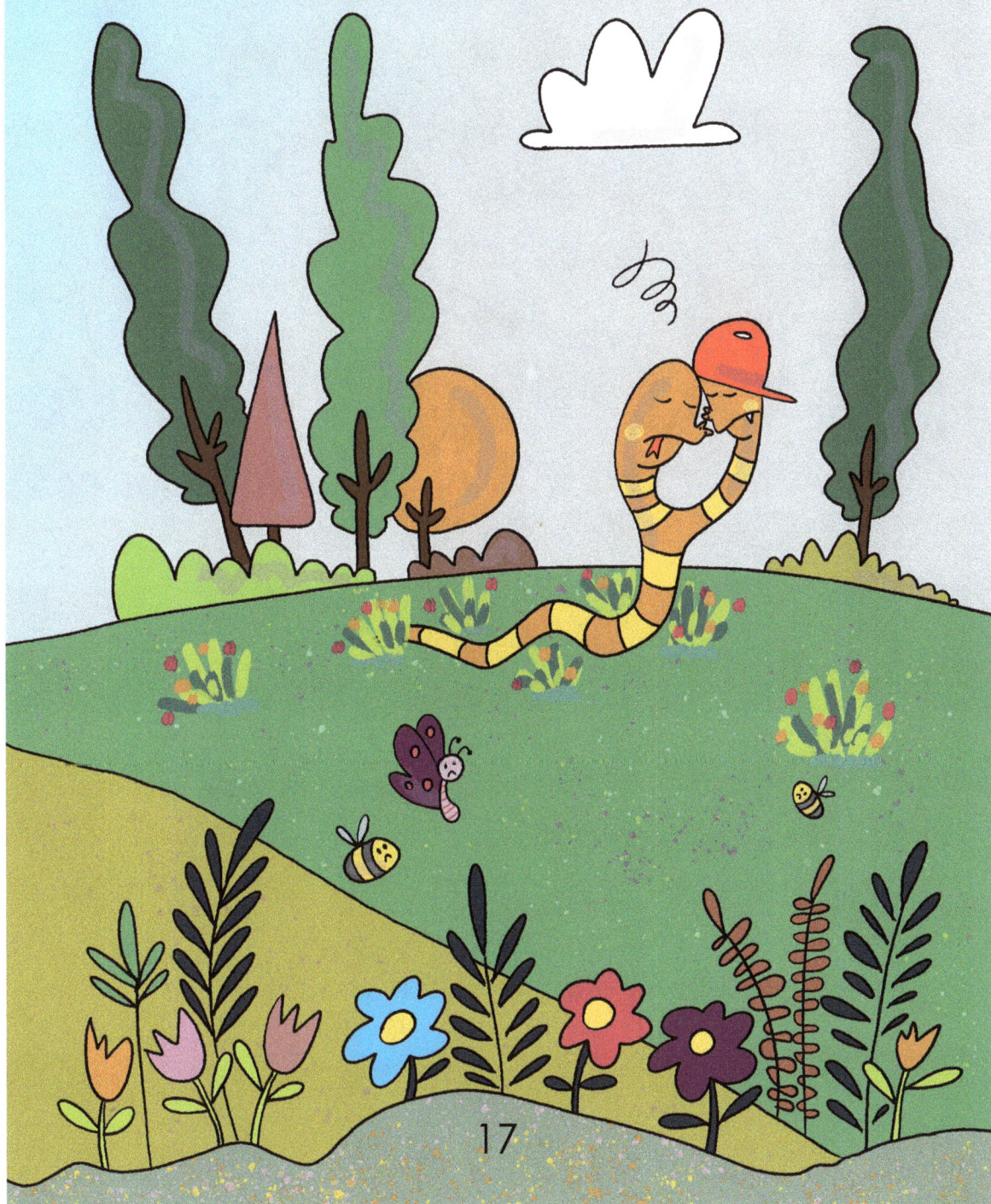

He coiled along the ground turning his heads in all directions, he was sure to see anyone or anything before they saw him.

Snake Adder began to feel hungry and so thirsty, he felt a cool Breeze blowing over his heads.

"Breeze is here!" shouted snake Adder.
And maybe Wind is on his way.

He had hoped Wind would blow him far away as a favour, or he would pay him back when he became more settled. After all, his moving was not planned.

Snake Adder knew Wind, did not always
blow from the same direction,
sometimes he would blow in a direction
you did not want to go.

Snake Adder remembered his brother Python, telling him how Wind had picked him up and blew him into Fire, at the Neptune Circus and another time in the Ocean, which was not very helpful.

Snake Adder also wanted to ask Breeze,
if the West Wind was heading his way.

He changed his mind, Breeze
sometimes did not want to
answer questions.

How big headed Breeze was,
thought snake.

Snake Adder then saw himself in a puddle, which made him smile.

I am a fine one to talk he thought.

27

I too have two big heads, but I am not poisonous and...

...no other snake looks like me!

The end